Make Me Musical
A Complete Music Education For
Kids

by David Harp

Dedication: I would like to dedicate this book to the two most important people in my life. Firstly, to my wife, Rita Ricketson, for her help and support on every conceivable level, without which this book could not have been written. And secondly, to our newest collaborative project, Katherine Grace Ricketson Harp (or "Katie", as she's known to her friends), just for being here.

© 1989 by David Harp. All Rights Reserved
Musical I Press, Inc.
PO Box 460908, San Francisco, California 94146

Printed by Spilman Printing of Sacramento, California

Contents

Introduction: For Grown Up Helpers Only

The above heading is a joke. I assume from experience (my own and that of other kids) that this section will be the first thing that many young readers will turn to, if only because it's not *supposed* to be for them. In fact, some children may want to read all of the Grown Up Helper sections throughout the book. Although I have presented the material using three different levels of reading in this book, younger readers are most welcome to tackle the more advanced instruction levels, and this book is programmed to encourage them to do so.

The large type sections, for young readers, present a simplified version of what is covered in the smaller typed sections for older readers. The Grown Up Helpers sections at the end of most lessons present hints for adults who are working with very young children.

Nina and David, Age Five

Very young kids will also enjoy and learn from the many pictures as they listen to the tape or their Grown Up reads the text to them.

However, I'll let my special guest foreword writer, Dr. Nina S. Feldman, explain the way that this book is organized, and why. Explaining such things is right up her alley, as she is a developmental psychologist, as well as a kid at heart.

Nina, after getting degrees in psychology from Vassar and Princeton, has taught at the University of Maryland and worked as a research psychologist for an international marketing firm. She now cogitates for a living at a think tank in Washington, D.C.

I'll let Nina introduce me. She's also rather well qualified to do that, having made a lifetime hobby out of being my twin sister.

Foreword: Nina Feldman, Ph.D.

Although it might be entertaining to spend some time here telling Dave stories (like the terrible thing he did to his cello in fifth grade, or how he drove everyone crazy in his first year of college with his harmonica), I'll focus instead on how he developed the methods used in this package.

David has been teaching harmonica to adults and children for fifteen years. When he decided to write the "definitive" children's harmonica book, he did two things.

He began to study other methods for teaching music to children, eventually focusing on the popular and effective Suzuki, Yamaha, and Orff-Schulwerk programs. To his satisfaction, he found that he was already using many of the techniques stressed in these methods.

In accord with Dr. Suzuki's wonderful work (mostly with violin), David emphasizes the role of the parent in working with very young children (ages two or three to five or six). If your young friend is in this age range, we strongly suggest that you take the time to learn to play a bit of harmonica yourself. Even if you've always considered yourself "unmusical", half an hour with this package will have you playing more music than some of you may ever have attempted. Just relax, take a short break from self-criticism, and allow yourself to discover an exciting new way of expressing yourself! Once you've learned to play just a bit, please feel free to create any variations of David's exercises, or new ones for you and your young friend to enjoy.

Learning a new skill with a child is much more than entertainment for both of you —it is a meeting on common ground. The ability to make both music and mistakes together is invaluable, and a wonderful opportunity to expose a very human side of yourself to your child, a side that many of us these hectic days have little time for. Try not to be goal-oriented — the point of this package is not only to make good music, it is to instill a love of music in the child. And instilling a love of music can help to instill self-esteem as well. As Dr. Suzuki says, the talent for music is innate in us all. As he beautifully expresses in the title of his invaluable book, this innate talent needs only to be "Nurtured By Love".

David also uses themes and techniques in common with the Orff-Schulwerk method. He teaches non-instrumental skills first, listening and moving to the music, rhythm play, ear-training for song familiarity, and an introduction to music notation systems. On the emotional side, as David quotes Dr. Orff: "Never criticize. Instead, help and correct." Or, as Dr. Suzuki puts it: "First do it. *Then* do it beautifully." (Italics mine.)

Although my baby brother avoids using psychological jargon or technical terms in his program, he did spend quite a bit of time picking my brain on appropriate subjects in developmental psychology. By studying the renowned Swiss psychologist Piaget, he gained an understanding of what children can do at different ages. For example, knowing that research indicates that children develop a sense of rhythm before they develop a sense of pitch (highness or lowness of sound) allowed him to create enjoyable and satisfying rhythm exercises for younger kids that lead into the melodic exercises for older kids.

Piaget's concepts of assimilation (learning to understand or work with new ideas or objects by applying already learned behaviors to them) and accomodation (learning how to deal with a new object or idea) helped David to teach the foundations of music in a progressive fashion. The earlier exercises prepare for the later ones. For example, the rhythm games will eventually allow the child to create his or her own blues style improvisation. And the dancing that the children do to David's sweet version of *Twinkle Twinkle Little Star* in Lesson Number Two will both encourage and prepare them to play the song by ear and harmonica notation, and eventually to read the important universal language of standard music notation.

In line with psychologists' concept of synesthesia (the act of transforming an experience from one sensory mode to another), David helps children to experience various feelings while listening to (and playing) the happy sounds of the major scale, the pensive sounds of the minor scale, and the mixed musical messages of the blues scale. He teaches them to visualize the train as it goes faster or slower, comes closer or goes away.

David's makes it excitingly clear that the harmonica is a practical, endlessly entertaining hobby, and an instant icebreaker in any social situation. But his underlying message is that music is a powerful tool for learning about oneself and one's feelings, a tool for expressing any type of emotions. The maturing child will find this method to be a royal road to the realm of imagination and symbolic expression.

By presenting both the classics and the study of free improvisation, David exposes the child to both the fabulous diversity of musical literature and to the immense potential of personal creativity through music. Although his package is a lifetime admission to the wonderful world of music, it is even more than that. It is about living joyously and openly in the larger world. As Groos said, play is "preparation for life." We believe that the same could be said for the playing of music. Enjoy!

Lesson One: How To Use This Book

Hi! My name is David Harp.
I want to teach you how to play the harmonica.

Playing harmonica is fun.

It is easy, too.

Are you in first grade, or in second, or third?

You can just read the words that are written in big letters.

Sometimes it is easier to learn about music by listening. So I would also like you to listen to Lesson Number One on the tape cassette. Please turn the tape on right now!

If you're an older kid, or if you like to read a lot, you can read these smaller words also. This book is designed so that both older and younger kids can use it to learn about music. You bigger kids may think that the sections written in big letters are too easy, but that's okay.

You should read them anyway. And I promise that I'll give you lots of more complicated information in these sections that are written in smaller letters. If this whole book seems pretty easy, that's okay too. When you are finished using this book and tape cassette, you will be ready to use the other books and tapes that I have made for teenagers and grownups.

If you want, you can also read the little words at the end of each lesson. These are instructions for parents or teachers who want to help kids who can't read yet, like four or five-year-olds. Maybe you would enjoy teaching a younger kid to play the harmonica. Teaching someone else can be the best way to learn!

No matter how old you are, it is really important to listen to the cassette tape *while* you read the book. There are two different ways to do that. You can read each lesson, and then listen to the lesson on the tape. Or you can listen to the lesson first, and then read about it. Try it both ways. Which works best for you?

Grownup Helpers: Read the large type section to your young friend, while pointing out the pictures of me, my harmonica, and the tape deck. If necessary, help the child put the tape in the deck and begin to play Side One, Lesson One.

Lesson Two: Why I Love To Play The Harmonica

I really love to play my harmonica.
I play it everywhere
that I go.
You can, too!
In front of the
campfire.
Or while
waiting for the
bus.

I want to play two songs for you right now.
Do you like to dance?

You can dance
while I play my
songs.

Please listen to
Lesson Number
Two on the tape
right now.

3

The harmonica can be used to play many different types of music. The two songs that I will play in Lesson Two are very different from each other. One is an old favorite, *Twinkle Twinkle Little Star*.

The other one is a song that I made up. It doesn't even have a name. It is a very special type of music called a **blues improvisation**. I would like to tell you more about these two words, blues and improvisation.

The **blues** are a type of music that was first created by the slaves who lived in the South of the United States just before the Civil War. The slaves remembered many songs that they had sung in Africa. When they came to the United States, they also learned many songs that the Americans had brought over from Europe. They combined these African and European styles of music, and invented the blues. Jazz music and rock and roll music are types of music that are based on the blues.

Improvisation means that the song is being made up while it is being played. Have you ever made up a story while you were telling it? Making up a story while you tell it is a little bit like making up a blues song while you are playing it. You don't really have time to *think* about what you are doing. You just have to *do* it, and hope that it comes out alright. Another word for improvisation is **jamm**. Sometimes two or more musicians improvise together. That is called a **jamm session**. I'll teach you how to improvise songs on the harmonica in Lesson Number Nine. Then we will have a jamm session together!

Please listen to my songs now. It is very important to listen to music, if you want to learn how to play. How do these songs make you feel? Does each song make you feel a different way?

Lesson Three: Your Harmonica

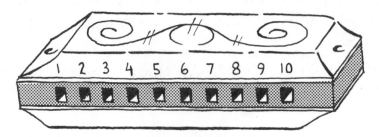

Look at your harmonica. Pick it up.

Count the little holes. Are there ten of them?

Can you   see the little numbers on your harmonica?

Hold your harmonica just like a sandwich.

Make sure that the numbers are on top.

You can use one hand or two hands to hold your harmonica.

Put your mouth over some of the little holes.

Breathe **out** through your harmonica.

Breathe **in** through your harmonica.

Sometimes the harmonica is called "the tin sandwich". Can you guess why? In Lesson Number Four I will tell you how the harmonica produces sound. For now, just make some sounds of your own.

Grown Up Helpers: Make sure that your friend can tell the difference between breathing in and breathing out. The taped directions in Lesson Three will help.

Lesson Four: Making Different Sounds

Some sounds are called "high" sounds.

Put your mouth over holes number 8, 9, and 10. Breathe in and out to make some high sounds.

Some sounds are called "low" sounds. Now put your mouth over holes number 1, 2, and 3. Breathe in and out again to make some low sounds.

Can you hear the difference?

I will help you teach your ears to hear better.

This is called "ear training".

Please listen to Lesson Number Four now.

Then you can play along with me!

Before I tell you about how the harmonica produces sound, I would like to teach you more about sound. I'll teach you more about sound by telling you a little story about a bumblebee. A story that seems to be about one thing but which teaches us about another thing is called an **analogy**. My bumblebee analogy will help you to understand how we hear sounds.

Imagine a bumblebee that has fallen into a swimming pool. Its wings **vibrate**, which means that they move back and forth very quickly. The vibration of the bumblebee's wings makes tiny waves in the water. A leaf near the edge of the pool will begin to move back and forth when the tiny waves reach it. The waves will make the leaf vibrate at the same speed as the bee's wings are vibrating.

Whenever *anything* vibrates, it creates tiny waves in the air. It doesn't matter what is vibrating. The head of a great big drum vibrates when we hit it with a drumstick. The string of a violin vibrates when we pluck it. The vocal cords inside our throats vibrate when we force air through them. A mosquito's wings vibrate as it flies. All of these vibrations create waves that flow through the air.

The big drum vibrates at a low speed, and sends big, slow waves through the air. The mosquito's wings vibrate at a very high speed, and send tiny, fast waves through the air.

When these vibrations reach the sensitive pieces of skin called **eardrums** inside our ears, they make the eardrums move back and forth at the same speed as whatever is vibrating, just like the bumblebee's wings made the leaf vibrate.

A very complicated set of bones, organs, and nerves connect our eardrums to our brain. They send a message to our brain that tells our

brain that our eardrums are vibrating. This message also tells our brain how fast our eardrums are vibrating. When our eardrums are vibrating very slowly, our brain lets us know that we are hearing what we call a **low** sound, like the sound that the big drum makes. When our eardrums are vibrating very quickly, our brain lets us know that we are hearing what we call a **high** sound, like the sound that the mosquito makes.

Musicians use a special word to talk about the highness or lowness of a sound. That word is **pitch**. High-pitched means a sound that is high. Low pitched means a sound that is low.

Our brain can only understand the messages carried by the bones and nerves when our eardrums are not vibrating too slowly or too quickly. This means that we cannot hear sounds when our eardrums are moving back and forth less than 20 times in each second. If our eardrums are vibrating more than 20,000 times each second, we cannot hear sounds. A dog's brain can understand the message when its eardrums are vibrating as fast as 40,000 times each second. That is why a dog can hear a dog whistle that creates vibrations as fast as 40,000 times a second, but we can't.

We can train our ears to hear the differences between higher notes and lower notes more easily. We will be doing lots of ear training with our tape cassette.

Inside each of the ten holes of our harmonica are two thin metal strips called **reeds**. Our out breath makes one of these reeds vibrate to produce a sound. Our in breath makes the other reed vibrate to produce a sound. The reeds in the lower end of the harmonica are bigger and vibrate slowly. They make sounds of a lower pitch than the smaller, faster reeds in the higher end of the harmonica. Here is a picture of the "in" reeds of your harmonica.

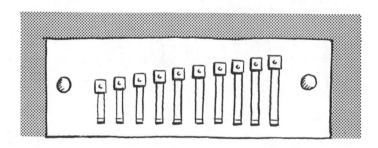

Grown Up Helpers: Your young friend does not need to know sound theory in order to play music. But he or she may enjoy listening to this section anyway!

Lesson Five: Writing Music Down

People who play music are called musicians.

Musicians have special ways to write music down on paper.

Look at some of the different ways of writing music on this page and page 12.

Now I would like to teach you how to read music that is written down for the harmonica.

This type of written music is called "harmonica tablature".

Please listen to Lesson Number Five on the tape.

Then look at the music on page 12 again.

Don't forget to play some more!

Musicians all around the world use a way of writing down music called the **standard notation** method. This way of writing down music was invented in Europe in the middle ages.

In standard notation, we use little pictures to represent sounds. If we wanted to write down the sound made by blowing in on one hole of our harmonica, it might look like this.

If we wanted to write down the sound made by blowing on three holes of our harmonica, it might look like this.

When we play just one sound at a time, the sound is called a **note**. When we play more than one note at a time, the sound is usually called a **chord**. You were playing chords on your harmonica when you blew in and out on the 1, 2, and 3 holes and on the 8, 9, and 10 holes.

When you play chords, your mouth is open wide, as if you were eating a popsicle.

Would you like to try playing just one note on your harmonica? You will have to breathe into just one hole at a time. Try making a very small opening with your mouth, as if you wanted to drink through a straw. Then put your mouth over hole number 1 or hole number 10, and breathe in or out. Holes number 1 and 10 are the easiest to play by themselves. There is no hole number 0 or hole number 11 to get in the way!

Sometimes musicians like to use a way of writing music down called **tablature**. Tablature is different for each instrument. When I write harmonica tablature, I tell you the holes that I want you to breathe through. I also tell you to breathe in or to breath out. Can you play me these notes?

1   **4**   **10**

out   **out**   **out**

If I want you to breathe through more than one hole at the same time, I put a line under the numbers. Can you play these three chords by reading the tablature?

1 2 3   **4 5 6**   **8 9 10**

out   **in**   **out**

I will teach you more about harmonica tablature in Lesson Six. I will teach you more about standard notation in Lesson Sixteen. Please listen to Lesson Number Five on the tape now, if you did not listen to the tape before you read this chapter.

Lesson Six: A Steady Beat

Listen to a clock.

Tick tick tick tick tick.

Take a walk, and listen to your feet.

Step step step step step step step step.

Clocks and feet can make a special type of sound.

This type of sound is called a "steady beat".

I'll tell you more about steady beats on the tape.

We will also clap our hands and march together.

Maybe we will dance, too!

Please listen to Lesson Number Six now.

Why is the clock's ticking like the sound of your feet when you walk? Because every tick and each step takes the same amount of time as every other tick or step. It is very important to keep a steady beat when we play music. Please look at the little rhythms and pictures of feet on the next page. Each little picture of a foot tells you to tap your foot. Each little picture of hands (clapping) tells you to clap. Can you sing the rhyme and tap your foot or clap at the same time like I do on the tape?

Sometimes we say one word with each tap or clap, like "one two three four". Sometimes we say more than one word with each tap or clap, like "one potato two potatoes three potatoes four". When we say more than one word for each tap we are making a **rhythm** along with our steady beat.

Sometimes I like to use a dot • to let you know when to tap your foot, instead of a picture of a foot. Please try to get used to tapping your foot whenever you see a dot.

It is hard to tell you about steady beats and rhythms in words. But it is easy to tell you about on tape. So please listen to Lesson Six now, if you have not listened to it already.

1	one	two	three	four	one	two	three	four

2	one potato	two potatoes	three potatoes	four

3						

4	• dirty	• dirty	• dog	•	• dirty	• dirty	• dog	•

5	• dirty	• dirty	• ding	• dong	• dog	• • •

Grown Up Helpers: Encourage your youngster to say the rhythms or dance along with them, even if he or she cannot tap or clap accurately. Like everything else, rhythm comes with practice.

Lesson Seven: The Train Song

Put your mouth over holes number 1, 2, and 3.

Now talk through your harmonica.

Say "One two three four". Does it sound funny?

Now say anything through the high end of your harmonica.

Now move the harmonica around while you talk through it.

Can you say "Chugga Chugga" through your harmonica?

Please listen to my train song in Lesson Seven.

Soon you will be playing a train song, too.

All aboard! Hear the whistle blow!

15

When we talk, we use our lips and our tongues to control the air from our lungs as it comes through our mouths. Say "tah". Can you feel your tongue push up against the top of your mouth before you say the "tah"? Can you feel your tongue drop down so that the "tah" can pop out? Using your tongue to control the air flow from your lungs is called **articulation**. Articulation lets us make lots of interesting sounds on the harmonica. We can articulate while we breathe in or out.

Most people think that it is harder to articulate while breathing in. Empty out all of the air from your lungs, and try to talk while you inhale. Do not let air come in through your nose. Can you do it? Is it hard? Please listen to Lesson Number Seven now.

Here is my train song, written out in harmonica tablature. Remember, each dot • means that you should tap your foot once.

•	•	•	•	•	•	•	•
123	**123**	**123**	**123**	**123**	**123**	**123**	**123**
In	**In**	**Out**	**Out**	**In**	**In**	**Out**	**Out**

Can you say "chugga" on each out chord? Try it! Can you say "chugga" on each in and each out chord? That's pretty hard to do. Don't worry if you cannot do it yet!

Every train needs to have a whistle. You can make a whistle for your train by putting your lips over the holes number 4 and 5. Then breathe in for two beats. Rest for two beats, then do it again. This is what my whistle looks like in harmonica tablature.

••	••	••	••
45		**45**	
In		**In**	

Are you ready to put the train and the whistle together? This is what the train and whistle look like in harmonica tablature.

•	•	•	•	••	••	••	••
123	**123**	**123**	**123**	**45**		**45**	
In	**In**	**Out**	**Out**	**In**		**In**	

Grown Up Helpers: Let your young friend make any sounds that feel "train-like" to them. And make sure that they try to imagine that train, while listening to it.

Lesson Eight: Playing By Yourself

Would you like to make up a song?
Listen to my made-up song
in Lesson Eight on the tape.
I only use the breathing out
notes. Now

you make

up a song!

Do you remember what I said in Lesson Number Two about improvising? Improvising means making up a song as we go. The easiest way to improvise is to only use the out notes of your harmonica. When Mr. Hohner invented the harmonica back in the 1830's, he made it so that all the out notes would form chords. That means that all of the out notes sound good together. That's why it is easy to improvise using only the out notes. Later on I'll teach you to improvise using all of the notes.

Grown Up Helpers: Listen to this section, and make up a song to play to your friend! It's easy!

Lesson Nine: Our First Jamm Session

Let's play together!
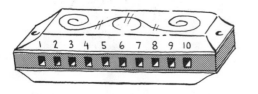

I have a musical instrument called a synthesizer.

It is like an electronic piano.

I will play some music on my synthesizer.

You can jamm along with me.

You only need to play the out notes.

I will tell you how in Lesson Nine on the tape.

Please listen to Lesson Nine before you read any more. Then jamm along with me. I don't want to talk about jamming any more right now. I just want to play some music — with you!

Grown Up Helpers: Make sure that your friend talks along with my articulations before starting to play. Then make sure that they are only breathing out, if possible.

Lesson Ten: Our Second Jamm Session

Let's have another jamm session!

This time you only need to play the in notes.

You will use the in notes from holes number 4, 5, 6, 7, 8, 9, and 10.

This jamm session will sound different from our first jamm session.

Please listen to Lesson Number Ten on the tape now.

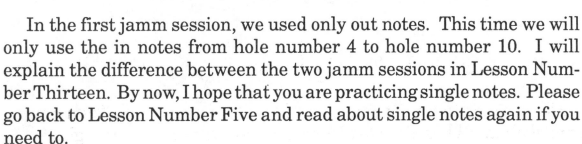

In the first jamm session, we used only out notes. This time we will only use the in notes from hole number 4 to hole number 10. I will explain the difference between the two jamm sessions in Lesson Number Thirteen. By now, I hope that you are practicing single notes. Please go back to Lesson Number Five and read about single notes again if you need to.

Grown Up Helpers: The "in" jamm is harder than the "out" jamm. Encourage your young friend to exhale lots of air when he or she gets filled up. Then they will have lots of in breath to play with.

Lesson Eleven: One More Jamm

Let's have one more jamm session!

Now you will play out notes and in notes together.

I will teach you a new in and out breathing rhythm.

| • | • | • | • | • | • | • | • | • | • | • | • |
| In | Out | In | Out | In | | In | Out | In | Out | In | |

| • | • | • | • | • | • | • | • • • |
| In | Out | | In | Out | | In | | Out | In | |

Then you can use it anywhere on your harmonica!

Please listen to Lesson Eleven on the tape now.

Lesson Twelve: The History Of Music

The harmonica is a very new musical instrument.

It is only 160 years old.

Some instruments are more than 10,000 years old. The drum is probably the oldest instrument.

A very smart man named Pythagoras lived in Greece more than 2,000 years ago.

He began to study sound and music.

We still use some of his ideas about music today.

I will tell you about some of Pythagoras' ideas.

I will tell you all about "octave notes".

I will also tell you about "scales".

Please listen to Lesson Number Twelve now.

People who study music are called **musicologists**. The study of music goes back a long way. We don't really know who the first musicologist was. Some people might say that the first musicologist was a caveman or cave woman who listened to the song of a bird and tried to

imitate it. Other people might say that the first musicologist was the person who discovered that hitting a hollow log with a stick made a nice, loud sound. We will probably never know for sure. What do you think?

We do know that Pythagoras was the first musicologist whose ideas were written down. Pythagoras was very interested in the sounds made by vibrating strings. He watched hunters hunting with bows and arrows, and listened to the sounds that the bowstrings made.

Lots of people had already realized that the "twang" of a tightened bow string made a higher sound than the "twang" of a loose bowstring. You can prove this for yourself by stretching a rubber band and pluck-

ing it. The tighter that the rubber band is, the higher the sound it makes.

Pythagoras began to experiment with different lengths of string. He discovered something very exciting. He found out that pluck-ing a string two feet long made a note that was very similar to the note he made by plucking a string one foot long. Then he learned that pluck-ing a string four feet long made a note that was similar to plucking a string two feet long. He wondered why strings that were one foot long, two feet long, four feet long, and even eight feet long all made notes that sounded similar.

Pythagoras realized that there was something very special about the notes that he got by plucking one string was half as long as the other. He

could hear that the notes they made were very similar. You can hear these similar notes too, if you listen to Lesson Number Twelve on the cassette. These similar notes are called **octaves,** or **octave notes**.

Do you remember that sound is produced by vibration? If you don't, please read Lesson Number Four again. Today we understand that a string one foot long vibrates exactly twice as fast as a string two feet long. A string two feet long vibrates exactly twice as fast as a string four feet long. No matter how long a string is, another string half as long will always vibrate twice as fast. And whenever something is vibrating exactly twice as fast as something else, the two sounds will always be similar. The two sounds will be octave sounds, or octave notes. Musicologists did not discover this fact until after the year 1700 A.D.

The harmonica can play four different octave notes. Have you begun to practice playing single notes? Then you can play some octave notes! Here are four octave notes on your harmonica. Under each note, I have written down how fast that reed is vibrating. The abbreviation "vps" means vibrations per second. Are you good at arithmetic? Then you can see that each one vibrates twice as fast as the one before it.

1	4	7	10
Out	Out	Out	Out
260 vps	520 vps	1040 vps	2080 vps

Pythagoras lived more than 2,000 years before 1700 A.D. So he did not know *why* the notes from his two foot string and his one foot string were similar. But he could hear that they sounded similar. He also realized that there were lots of different notes that could fit in between the higher octave note of his one foot string and the lower octave note of his two foot string.

Pythagoras wanted to find out which of these in-between sounds fit in best. He decided to use fractions, like 1/2 and 1/3 and 1/4, to help him find the right notes. Have you studied fractions yet? If you do not know fractions, it will be hard to understand the

next two paragraphs. But you will still be able to play lots of music, so don't worry.

The ancient Greeks already liked to use fractions in their art. The wrist of a Greek statue was always one-half (1/2) as big around as the neck of a Greek statue. The head of a Greek statue was always one-seventh (1/7) as long as the body of a statue. They used many other fractions in their art. They also used fractions when

they made their buildings. So it was natural for Pythagoras to want to use fractions in his study of music.

Pythagoras knew that cutting the length of a string in half could be written down as the fraction one-half. He wondered if cutting the length of a string by other fractions would make sounds that also seemed similar. He compared the sounds of a string three feet long, and a string one foot long. These two strings could be written down mathematically as the fraction one-third, or 1/3. He also experimented with lots and lots of other string lengths and fractions.

Eventually Pythagoras decided that there were eleven notes that seemed to fit best in between the higher octave note of his one foot string and the lower octave note of his two foot string. He used these notes to divide up the musical distance between the higher octave note and the lower octave note. No one today knows exactly why he choose the sounds that he did.

Musicologists use a special word to describe the way that the musical distance between two octave notes is divided up by the in-between notes. That word is **scale**. Pythagoras' way of dividing up this musical distance was called the **chromatic scale**. There are many different ways to divide up the musical distance between the higher octave note and the lower octave note. So there are many different scales. Pythagoras' chromatic scale is the earliest scale that we know about. It is still used today in almost all of the music that we play.

When we talk about a scale, we usually include the lower octave note and the higher octave note as well as the notes in-between. So the scale invented by Pythagoras had 13 notes. There was one lower octave note, the 11 in-between notes, and one higher octave note (1 + 11 + 1 = 13).

I will show you a way of drawing Pythagoras' scale. It looks a little like a staircase. Since Pythagoras divided the distance between higher octave note (top line) and the lower octave note (bottom line) into equal pieces, all of the steps are the same height.

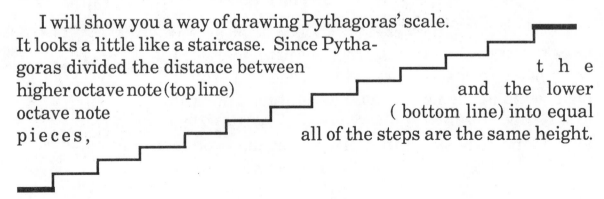

Please look at my picture of a piano or synthesizer keyboard. Most pianos have eight chromatic scales. Some synthesizers have only four or five chromatic scales. If you look very carefully, you will see that there is a repeated pattern of white and black notes. We can begin a chromatic scale on any note. We then count up or down thirteen white and black notes to locate one chromatic scale on the piano. We must remember to count the notes that we start and end on. This will be easier to do in the next lesson when we give letter names to the notes of the scale.

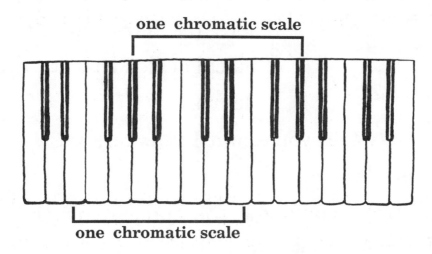

Your harmonica does not have all the notes of the chromatic scale. Your harmonica uses a simpler scale called the **major scale**. The major scale is based on Pythagoras' chromatic scale. I'll tell you more about this in the next chapter.

Grown-ups: This lesson will probably be too difficult for young children to understand. But they should listen to the taped sections, and perhaps try to play the harmonica octave notes described above and demonstrated on the tape.

Lesson Thirteen: More Music History

Musical scales are a lot like alphabets.

We use the letters of an alphabet to make sentences.

We use the notes of a scale to make up songs.

There are four different musical scales that we need to learn.

I have already told you about Pythagoras' chromatic scale.

Now I will teach you about the major scale, the minor scale and the blues scale.

Please listen to Lesson Number Thirteen now.

It may be easier for you to understand the rest of this lesson if you listen to the cassette first. Then you will know how the different scales sound while you read about them.

There are many different types of scales. But almost all American music can be played using only four scales. These are the **chromatic scale**, the **major scale,** the **minor scale** and the **blues scale.**

All music is based on scales, just like all writing is based on alphabets. The 26 letters of the English alphabet, from A to Z, give us the basic building blocks to make up words and sentences and books. If we use different combinations of the Japanese alphabet, we make up Japanese words and sentences and books. If we use different combinations of the Russian alphabet, we make up Russian words and sentences and books.

The notes of a musical scale are like the letters of an alphabet. We can use the notes of a scale in any combination to make up songs or parts of songs. If we use the notes of the major scale, we will create a song that sounds a particular way. If we use the notes of a minor scale, we will create a song that sounds a different way. If we use the notes of a blues scale, we will create a song that sounds different from the major song and the minor song.

Do you remember the songs that we made up in lessons number nine and ten? In lesson number nine, we used all of the out notes. The major scale uses all of these out notes. Our out note jamm sounded happy and bouncy. In lesson number ten we used the in notes from hole 4 to hole 10. The minor scale uses lots of high in notes. Our in note jamm sounded a little more sad or wistful. These two jamms sounded different because we were building them, or **composing** them, out of different notes. Now I will tell you about the history of the major scale, the minor scale, and the blues scale.

Although Pythagoras' chromatic scale was very popular, some people preferred to use scales that had less in-between notes. They experimented with leaving out some of the in-between notes that Pythagoras used. By the time of the middle ages, two of these simpler scales had become especially widely used.

One of these two simpler scales was called the **major scale**. The major scale used only six of Pythagoras' in-between notes, instead of eleven. So counting the lower octave note, the six in-between notes, and the upper octave note, each major scale had eight notes. Songs composed from the notes of the major scale had a very happy and grand sound.

The other of these two simpler scales was called the **minor scale**. The minor scale also used only six of Pythagoras' in-between notes, instead of eleven. So each minor scale also had eight notes. But some of the in-between notes used in the minor scale were different from the in-between notes used in the major scale. Songs composed from the notes of the minor scale have a much sadder sound than major scale songs. It is easy to hear the difference.

There is one more very important scale that I would like to tell you about. The **blues scale** is a bit of a mystery. Some musicologists believe that the blues scale existed in Africa a very long time ago. Other musicologists think that the blues scale was created after African people were brought to America as slaves. Since there were no tape recorders back then, we will never know who is right. But we do know that the African or Afro-American-based blues scale is used to compose almost all of the world's most popular music. Rock and roll music, jazz music, funk music, disco music, soul music, and of course blues music are all based on the blues scale!

The blues scale has only five in-between notes, so with the two octave notes each blues scale is made up of seven notes. The blues scale sounds "bluesy"—but I will let you hear that for yourself. Playing a blues scale on the harmonica requires "bending". Bending is a special way of breathing through the harmonica. It is not easy to do, but it sounds great. I'll talk more about bending in Lesson Number Fifteen.

Here are **"staircase"** pictures of the major scale, the minor scale, and the blues scale. You can see how the major, the minor, and the blues scales do not divide the distance between octave notes into equal distances. You can also see that even though the major and minor scales both have eight notes, the notes are not the same.

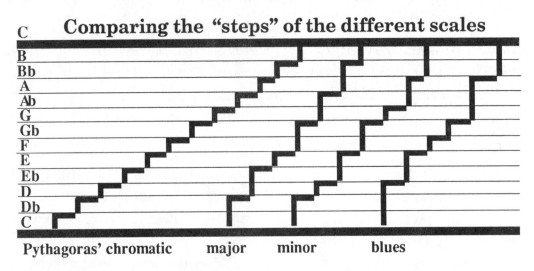

Comparing the "steps" of the different scales

Pythagoras' chromatic   major   minor   blues

In Lesson Fifteen we will learn to play a major scale and a major song on our harmonicas. In Lesson Eighteen we will learn to play a minor scale and a minor song on our harmonicas. Before we do that, I want to teach you about the letter names that we use to represent music notes.

Lesson Fourteen: Letter Names For Notes

Each music note has a letter name.

I will teach you the letter names of the notes on the piano and the harmonica.

The white notes on the piano are named A, B, C, D, E, F, and G.

Can you read the letter name of each white note?

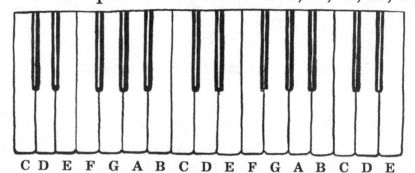

C D E F G A B C D E F G A B C D E

Our harmonicas use these same letter names.

Look at my chart of the harmonica letter names.

Please listen to Lesson Number Fourteen now.

Hole Number:		1	2	3	4	5	6	7	8	9	10
This note plays when you breathe:	In	D	G	B	D	F	A	B	D	F	A
This note plays when you breathe:	Out	C	E	G	C	E	G	C	E	G	C

Another important musical event had happened by the middle ages. Sometime around the year 1000 A.D., musicologists began to give letter names to the different music notes. By the time that the piano was invented, the letters A, B, C, D, E, F, and G were used to represent the white keys. Since the different octave notes sounded so much alike, the same letter name was used for all octave notes.

I am going to use another analogy to teach you about the names of the black keys. Do you remember that an analogy is a story that seems to be about one thing but which teaches us about another thing? Look at the picture of the piano. The lower notes are on the left side. The higher notes are to the right side. You can see that each of the black keys has a white key on both sides of it.

Here is my analogy. Pretend that you live in the house in the picture. If you wanted to describe your house without using your name, you could do it in two ways. You could say "the house uphill from the Jones house". Or you could say "the house downhill from the Smith house". Each black key also has two names that mean the same thing.

One letter name is called a **sharp** name. Sharp means "higher than". The sharp name tells us which white key the black key is a little bit higher than. So the black key named "A sharp" is the black key a little bit higher than A. Sometimes instead of the word "sharp" musicologists use the symbol #.

The other letter name is called a **flat** name. Flat means "lower than". The flat name tells us which white key the black key is a little bit lower than. So the black key named "B flat" is the black key a little bit lower than B. Sometimes instead of the word "flat" musicologists use the symbol b.

You can see that A sharp and B flat are exactly the same note. Please look at the picture of a piano with all the letter names for white and black notes. I have used the symbol # for sharp and b for flat.

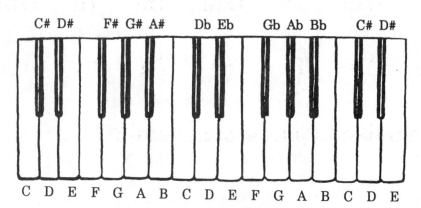

Look at the harmonica letter name chart on the page 29. The first note of our harmonica is the number 1 out note. This note has the letter name C. That is why our harmonica is called a C harmonica. Harmonicas are made starting on every note of the piano. Luckily for us, once we learn to play the C harmonica, we can play all the others too. Someday you may want to get an F sharp harmonica, or a B flat harmonica, or an A harmonica. I like to play them all!

Grown-ups: If your young friend knows the alphabet, let him or her point out the letter names of the white keys, and the letter names of the harmonica notes. Don't worry about the black key names at all, yet.

Lesson Fifteen: The Major Scale

Your harmonica is made to play a major scale.

I will show you how to play the easiest major scale.

I will write down the notes for you in harmonica tablature.

I will also write some words that people use to sing the major scale.

I will also write down the letter name of each note.

4	4	5	5	6	6	7	7
Out	In	Out	In	Out	In	In	Out
C	D	E	F	G	A	B	C
Do	Re	Me	Fa	So	La	Ti	Do

Would you like to play a major scale?

It is not too easy. Listen to me do it first.

Would you like to play *Twinkle Twinkle Little Star?*

Would you like to play *Skip To My Lou?*

I have written them down in harmonica tablature.

But please listen to Lesson Fifteen on the tape first.

Please practice playing the major scale on your harmonica now. Do not worry too much about playing single notes. Just try to aim at the holes that I have written down for the major scale. And make sure that you are breathing out and in at the right times. Some people get used to breathing out, then in on the number 4, 5, and 6 holes. Then they forget that they have to breathe in then out on hole number 7. Did that happen to you? After you learn to play the major scale, you will be able to play lots of different songs!

We can only play one major scale on our harmonica. We have C harmonicas. We will play a major scale starting on the C note of our harmonica. This major scale is called a C major scale.

If we had pianos, we could play major scales that began on any of the notes of the chromatic scale. We could play 12 different major scales. But we would have to learn to pick out the right white and black notes. These notes would be different for each of the 12 major scales.

Harmonicas are a bit like pianos that only have white keys. Of course, our harmonicas don't have any keys. But the notes that our harmonicas can play are the same as the notes of the white keys. Look at the chart of the harmonica notes on page 29. You will only see the notes C, D, E, F, G, A, and B.

You can see that there is only one place to play a complete C major scale on the harmonica. You can almost play one on holes number 1, 2, 3, and 4. But the F and A notes are missing. You can almost play one on holes number 7, 8, 9, and 10. But the B note is missing. If theses notes were not left out, it would be harder to play chords on the harmonica. So the inventor of the harmonica decided to leave them out.

Good harmonica players have a way to play the black notes of the piano on the harmonica. It is called **bending**. Bending is a special way of moving our tongue while we blow in or out on one of the holes. Bending lets us play the notes that are in-between the notes that we usually play. I have also written a whole book about bending, for people who want to learn to play very well. Bending is especially important for people who want to play blues music.

Why don't you try playing *Twinkle Twinkle Little Star* now. Play each line of the song a few times before you try to play the whole song. Remember to tap your foot every time you see a dot. Then play *Skip To My Lou*. Soon I will give you some other songs to play. But these are good songs to start with.

Twinkle Twinkle Little Star

•	•	•	•	•	•	••		•	•	•	•	•	•	••
Twin	kle	twin	kle	lit	tle	star		how	I	won	der	what	you	are
4	4	6	6	6	6	6		5	5	5	5	4	4	4
O	O	O	O	I	I	O		I	I	O	O	I	I	O

•	•	•	•	•	•	••		•	•	•	•	•	•	••
Up	a	bove	the	world	so	high		like	a	dia	mond	in	the	sky
6	6	5	5	5	5	4		6	6	5	5	5	5	4
O	O	I	I	O	O	I		O	O	I	I	O	O	I

•	•	•	•	•	•	••		•	•	•	•	•	•	••
Twin	kle	twin	kle	lit	tle	star		how	I	won	der	what	you	are
4	4	6	6	6	6	6		5	5	5	5	4	4	4
O	O	O	O	I	I	O		I	I	O	O	I	I	O

Skip To My Lou

••	••	•	•	•	•	••	••	•	•	•	•
Lou	Lou	skip	to	my	Lou	Lou	Lou	skip	to	my	Lou
5	4	5	5	5	6	4	3	4	4	5	5
O	O	O	O	O	O	I	I	I	I	I	I

••	••	•	•	•	•	•	•	•	•	••	•	•
Lou	Lou	skip	to	my	Lou	Skip	to	my	Lou	my	dar	ling
5	4	5	5	5	6	4	5	5	5	4	4	4
O	O	O	O	O	O	I	O	I	O	I	O	O

Grown Up Helpers: Help your young friend point to the *Do Re Mi Fa So La Ti Do* while I sing and play it on the tape. If they would like to try the major scale, help them to get the ins and outs right by doing them without the harmonica first.

It may be easier to begin *Twinkle Twinkle* by playing only the first two words of the song, as all four of the first notes are out notes. Just help them move the harmonica from the general area of the number 4 hole to the general area of the number 6 hole while saying "twinkle twinkle". When this feels comfortable, then try the rest of the first line.

Some children will find *Skip To My Lou* easier than *Twinkle Twinkle*. The following is a description of a very simplified version of *Skip To My Lou.* Have your friend place his or her mouth over the number 3, 4, and 5 holes. Then have them use the correct in and out breaths without moving their mouth from these holes. Have them say the words of the song through the harmonica. It is harder to do when breathing in. Remind them not to let air in through their noses when breathing in (pretend that they are drinking a milk shake through a straw).

A number of songs are written out in the next lessons. If your little friend was able to play all or part of *Twinkle Twinkle* or *Skip To My Lou,* encourage them to pick out more songs, even if they find the standard notation sections below difficult. They can always come back and learn standard notation later on. Remember: many famous and successful musicians never learn to use standard notation at all!

Lesson Sixteen: Another Way To Write Music

We now know how to write music in many ways.

We can write music in harmonica tablature.

We can write music with the letter names of our notes.

We can draw staircase pictures of our scales.

We can also use standard notation to write music.

Standard notation is a bit like the staircase pictures.

But we don't use steps to show the notes.

Instead, we use lines and spaces.

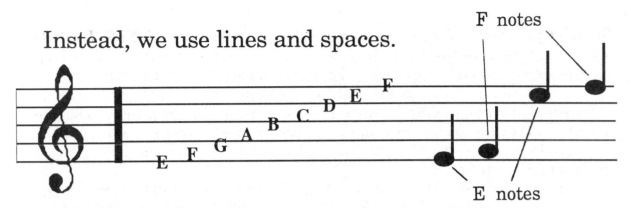

Each of the lines has a letter name.

Each of the spaces has a letter name.

To write down a note, we put a picture of a music note on one of the lines or spaces.

We put a high note up on one of the higher lines.

We put a low note down on one of the lower lines.

Now listen to Lesson Number Sixteen on the tape.

Learning to read standard notation is a little bit like learning to read a foreign language. At first it seems very strange. It has lots of rules, and some of them do not seem to make much sense. But when you get used to it, it seems very natural. Soon I will teach you a game that will help you to read standard notation just like you read the English language.

Many musicians cannot read standard notation. They just read harmonica tablature if they want to play harmonica. They read guitar tablature if they want to play guitar. Some musicians don't even read tablature. They just listen to a piece of music, and then try to play it. This is called "playing by ear".

Other musicians think that everyone should read standard notation. They think that a musician who can't read standard notation is like a person who can't read at all.

I think that it is good to be able to play all three ways. I would like you to learn to read harmonica tablature and standard notation. And I would like you to be able to play by ear also.

I only want to help you *get started* reading standard notation. Later on, there will be a lot more for you to learn about standard notation. For instance, we will only practice reading songs that use the C major scale in this book. They are the easiest standard notation songs to read. Some day you may want to learn how to read songs using all of the other scales. There are lots of other things that you may want to learn about standard notation after you have finished this book and tape.

The five lines and four spaces that we use to draw notes on are called the **staff**. There are two main types of staffs. The **upper** or **Treble Staff** is used to draw middle and high notes on. That is the kind of staff that we will use, because the harmonica does not have very low notes. Another kind of staff, called the **lower** or **Bass Staff**, is used when we want to draw very low notes, like the notes that a bass guitar plays. A picture called a **clef** is drawn at the beginning of each staff. The clef picture tells us whether that staff is a treble staff or a bass staff. I'll draw you a treble clef on the left, and a bass clef on the right.

pic of treble and bass clefs with a bit of staff

Not all of our harmonica notes will fit onto the five lines and four spaces of the treble staff. Some are too high, and some are too low. So musicians draw extra lines, called **leger lines** (sometimes spelled ledger lines), above and below the treble staff. We must draw two high leger lines, and four low leger lines to fit in all of our harmonica notes.

The following chart shows where each of your harmonica's notes are written on a treble staff. I have also written down the harmonica tablature names for each note under the staff. I have drawn a thin line connecting each letter name on the staff with each harmonica tablature name. Remember, two of the notes (F and A) in the low C major Scale and one of the notes in the high C major scale (B) are not built into the harmonica.

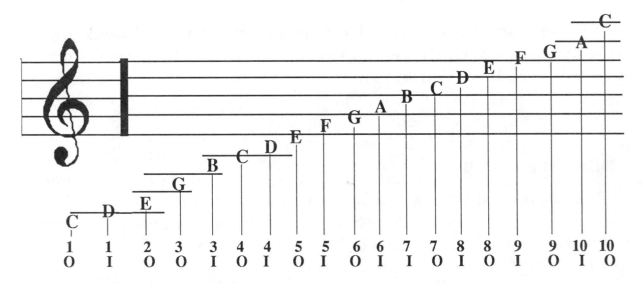

If you want to read standard notation, you will need to memorize the letter names of each line and space. Here is a game that will help you to do that. I will put some notes onto the staff. The letter names of the notes will spell out a word when you read them from left to right. I will give you the answers to the first three: face, beef, and egg. You will have to figure out the rest for yourself.

I will write out a whole sentence in standard notation. (I'll give you the answer at the end of this chapter, if you really can't figure it out). Can you make up some silly sentences of your own? By the way, you may notice some upright lines in between the notes on the staff. They are called bar lines, and I will explain them soon.

After you have begun to memorize the letter names of each line and space, you will also need to learn how to find each note on the harmonica when you see it written in standard notation. This will take some practice. Some notes are easier than others. For instance, it is easy to remember the number 5 hole breathing out. It is the note written on the bottom line of the staff. The in and out notes between holes number four and seven are the most important to learn, for now.

When I learned to read standard notation, my music teacher had us memorize the word F-A-C-E for the spaces from bottom to top, and the sentence E-very G-ood B-oy D-oes F-ine for the lines (E-G-B-D-F) from bottom to top. I always thought that was unfair to the girls! You can learn where the notes are any way that you like. I will write out some exercises that will help you.

Please play the two sets of notes that I have written down here in standard notation. The notes marked "out notes" are the out notes from hole number four to hole number seven. The notes marked "in notes" are the in notes from hole number four to hole number seven. You can see that the higher notes (like the number seven out) are drawn up higher, and that the lower notes (like number four out) are drawn down lower. Please look at the notation, listen to the sound, and feel where your mouth is on the harmonica as you do this exercise.

Please practice playing the major scale while you look at the standard notation for the major scale. If you do not already know the major scale, now is a good time to practice!

And look at the notation for the first line of *Twinkle Twinkle Little Star*. Can you see the notes jump up from the first "twinkle" to the second "twinkle"? Soon you will be playing this whole song from standard notation!

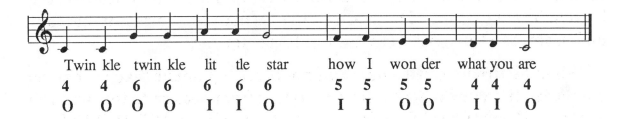

If you would like to play all of the lines and spaces of the staff, here is how to do it on the harmonica. If this seems hard or confusing, just stick to the "in notes" and the "out notes" exercises, and the major scale.

There is only one more thing about standard notation that you need to learn. In my harmonica tablature, I show how long to play each note by placing footprints or dots above the number of the hole. In standard notation, the way that a note is drawn tells how long to play that note.

There are four different types of notes that we must learn. A **whole note** looks like a flattened-out circle. Whenever we see a whole note, we know that we must hold that note for **four beats.** In some types of music a whole note does not equal four beats, but this is very unusual. So don't worry about it. If you do not remember how to count out a steady beat, please read and listen to Lesson Number Six again.

A **half note** looks like a whole note with a line called a **stem** attached to it. Whenever we see a half note, we know that we must hold that note for **two beats.** The stem of any note can point either up or down, whichever looks better to the writer.

A **quarter note** looks like a filled-in half note. Whenever we see a quarter note, we know that we must hold that note for **one beat**.

An **eighth note** looks like a quarter note with a little **flag** attached to the stem. Whenever we see an eighth note, we know that we must hold that note for **one half of a beat**. Sometimes when we have two or three eighth notes next to each other, we attach them with a **beam** instead of giving each one a separate flag.

We will not be using them, but there are also **sixteenth notes**. They have two flags. We hold sixteenth notes for **one quarter of a beat**.

NOTE		REST
♪ =	half a beat =	↗
♩ =	one beat =	≹
♩(half) =	two beats =	▬
○ =	four beats =	▄

Sometimes we just rest during a beat or two, and don't play anything at all. In harmonica tablature, I tell you to rest by drawing a dot that doesn't have a hole number or in/out under it. In standard notation, there are pictures that tell you to rest for one beat or two beats or four beats or one half of a beat. They are called **rests**. We will mostly use one beat rests.

When we write music in standard notation, we usually divide notes up into **bars** or **measures**. This makes them easier to read, instead of having lots of notes in one long line. One bar (or measure) is the area between the up and down bar lines. In most of the music that we play, each measure or bar will be four beats long. That means that if we count up all the notes in a bar, they will equal four beats. As you can see, four beats could be one whole note, or two half notes, or four quarter notes, or eight eighth notes. Four beats could also be one half note and four eighth notes, or two quarters, two eighths, and an eighth rest. Occasionally you will even see music divided into bars of three beats each.

One bar (between lines) ≡ 4 beats

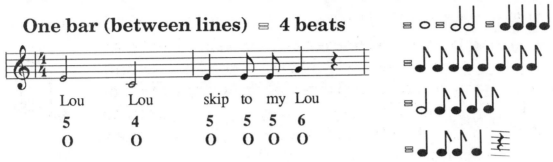

At the beginning of each staff, you will see two numbers, one on top of the other. They are called the **time signature**. The top number tells us how many beats are in each bar. This number will usually be a 4. Sometimes it will be a 3. Once in a while it will be a 2 or something else. The bottom number tells us how many beats make one whole note. This number is almost always 4, as I said before (one whole note = 4 beats).

Please practice saying the following rhythms through your harmonica while you look at the drawn notes and the numbers. They may look a bit scary or confusing. But they're old friends, the dirty dirty dogs! Then cover up the numbers and say the rhythms while you only look at the standard notation.

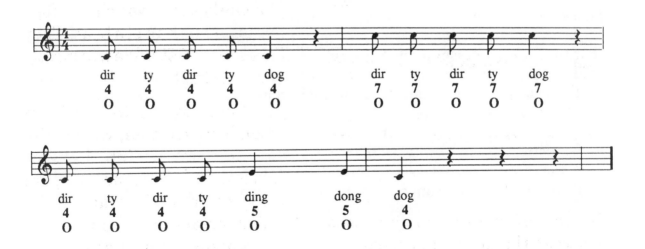

dir ty dir ty dog
4   4   4   4   5
O   O   O   O   O

dir ty dir ty dog
4   4   4   4   3
O   O   O   O   O

dir ty dir ty ding   dong dog
4   4 4   4 7   7   4
O   O O   O O   O   O

dog   dir ty dog
4   4   4 4
O   O   O O

dog   dir ty dog
5   5   5 5
O   O   O O

dir ty dir ty dir ty
7   7   7   7   7   7
O   O   O   O   O   O

doggg
4
O

Now you know enough about standard notation to start playing songs. Begin by just listening to me play *Skip To My Lou*, while you look at both the standard notation and the harmonica tablature. Then, if you feel ready, cover up the harmonica tablature and try playing the song while just looking at the standard notation. Eventually you will be able to look at a note on the staff and know exactly which hole to breathe into!

Grown Up Helpers: Please don't worry if your young friend seems uninterested in standard notation. It is *much* more important for him or her just to enjoy playing, or even listening. You might try pointing at the notes as I play the song (if you can't follow the notation, you can always look at the words of the song). Or just use the major scale and first line of *Twinkle Twinkle Little Star* as examples to demonstrate that the higher the sound, the higher the note is written on the staff.

Because the harmonica has so many high notes, we harmonica musicians often write down our notes as though the harmonica was one octave lower than it really is. This makes it easier to read the standard notation. We can write 8va (which means one octave lower) above the staff to let non-harmonica musicians know that we are doing this. But I will just mention it here, in case you noticed. If not, please don't worry about it, as it does not affect the notation or the playing in the slightest! **And the mystery sentence from page 37 is: A bad egg bagged a cabbage!**

Lesson Seventeen: Some Songs To Play

Please listen to me play some more songs for you.

You can look at the standard notation for these songs while you listen to them.

Play along with me if you want to!

Now that you can read music in two different ways, please try playing some of the following songs. I put the songs that I think are easier first. But everyone has his or her own ideas about what is easy and what is hard. So please try these songs in whatever order you want. Remember, the better you know a song, the easier it will probably be to play.

Please listen to each song on the tape as you read the notation. See if you can follow along note by note as I play, just like you can look at the words in a book whild someone is reading them. Sometimes, when you listen, just look at the rhythm part of the notation, and do not even think about which notes are being played. Other times, just look at where the notes are on the staff as you listen to them. It's exciting to begin to read standard notation! Just like learning a new language!

I have written these songs down as though we were playing them using only single notes. But if you can't get single notes too well, just aim at the single note that I have written, and let your mouth be as wide as it has to be. All of these songs will sound just fine if you need to use chords!

Eventually I would like you to try to play these songs using the standard notation, if you can. If you can't, use the harmonica tablature and just use the standard notation to find out how long to play each note. And if you listen to me play the songs on the tape, you may be able to play them yourself without even looking at any notation! It's fun to play by ear, sometimes!

Skip To My Lou is an old friend by now. Remember that eighth notes are played for one half of a beat, and don't forget to rest for one beat when you see the funny shaped rest notation. Look back at page 40 if you have forgotten what the notes and rests look like. Now go for it!

Lou	Lou	skip	to	my	Lou
5	4	5	5	5	6
O	O	O	O	O	O

Lou	Lou	skip	to	my	Lou
4	3	4	4	4	5
I	I	I	I	I	I

Lou	Lou	skip	to	my	Lou
5	4	5	5	5	6
O	O	O	O	O	O

Skip	to	my	Lou	my	dar	ling
4	5	5	5	4	4	4
I	O	I	O	I	O	O

Twinkle Twinkle Little Star is a wonderful song. But I've already played it twice. If you want to listen to it while you read, go to my fancy version in Lesson Two, or my simple one in Lesson Fifteen.

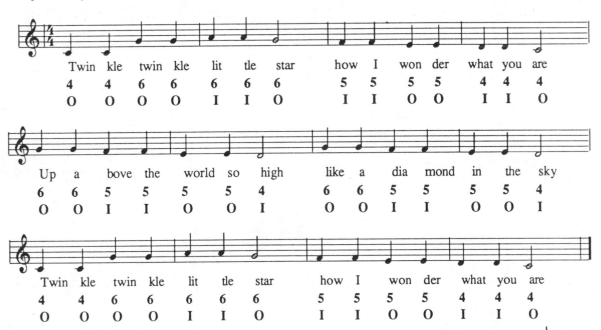

	Twin	kle	twin	kle	lit	tle	star	how	I	won	der	what	you	are
	4	4	6	6	6	6	6	5	5	5	5	4	4	4
	O	O	O	O	I	I	O	I	I	O	O	I	I	O

	Up	a	bove	the	world	so	high	like	a	dia	mond	in	the	sky
	6	6	5	5	5	5	4	6	6	5	5	5	5	4
	O	O	I	I	O	O	I	O	O	I	I	O	O	I

	Twin	kle	twin	kle	lit	tle	star	how	I	won	der	what	you	are
	4	4	6	6	6	6	6	5	5	5	5	4	4	4
	O	O	O	O	I	I	O	I	I	O	O	I	I	O

Clementine was a favorite song of the '49 ers in California. I mean the ones that came for the gold rush in 1849, not the football team! Did they really play harmonica while panning for gold? Who knows? But they could've, because the harmonica is the only instrument that you can play while you do anything else!

	Oh	my	dar	lin	oh	my	dar	lin	oh	my	dar	lin	Clem	en	tine
	4	4	4	3	5	5	5	4	4	5	6	6	5	5	4
	O	O	O	O	O	O	O	O	O	O	O	O	I	O	I

	you	are	lost	but	not	for	got	ten	oh	my	dar	lin	Clem	en	tine
	4	5	5	5	5	4	5	4	4	5	4	3	3	4	4
	I	O	I	I	O	I	O	O	O	O	I	O	I	I	O

Jingle Bells is no harder to play than *Skip To My Lou*. Just make sure that you've got lots of Out breath ready for those long whole notes!

Jin	gle	bells	jin	gle	bells	jin	gle	all	the	way
5	5	5	5	5	5	5	6	4	4	5
O	O	O	O	O	O	O	O	O	I	O

oh	what	fun	it	is	to	ride	on	a	one	horse	o	pen	sle	igh
5	5	5	5	5	5	5	5	5	5	4	4	5	4	6
I	I	I	I	I	O	O	O	O	O	I	I	O	I	O

Jin	gle	bells	jin	gle	bells	jin	gle	all	the	way
5	5	5	5	5	5	5	6	4	4	5
O	O	O	O	O	O	O	O	O	I	O

oh	what	fun	it	is	to	ride	on	a	one	horse	o	pen	sleigh
5	5	5	5	5	5	5	5	5	6	6	5	4	4
I	I	I	I	I	O	O	O	O	O	O	I	I	O

You Are My Sunshine is one of my favorite songs. The line that connects the last two notes is called a **tie**. It means that you play the two notes that it connects as though they were one long note. In this case, the long note is five beats long, since the tie connects a whole note (four beats) and a quarter note (one beat).

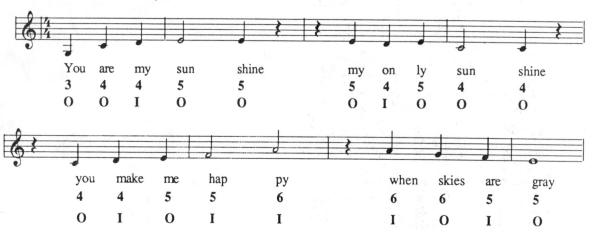

You	are	my	sun	shine	my	on	ly	sun	shine
3	4	4	5	5	5	4	5	4	4
O	O	I	O	O	O	I	O	O	O

you	make	me	hap	py	when	skies	are	gray
4	4	5	5	6	6	6	5	5
O	I	O	I	I	I	O	I	O

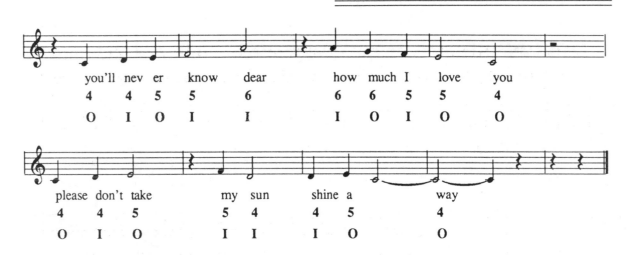

you'll	nev	er	know	dear		how	much	I	love	you
4	4	5	5	6		6	6	5	5	4
O	I	O	I	I		I	O	I	O	O

please	don't	take		my	sun	shine	a		way
4	4	5		5	4	4	5		4
O	I	O		I	I	I	O		O

The Farmer In The Dell has lots of eighth notes. This song may be easier to play by ear than from notation, at first. Do you know all the verses? There's one about the farmer, then about his wife, his child, his dog, his cat, a mouse and the cheese!

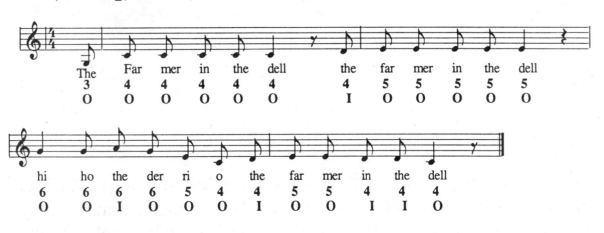

The	Far	mer	in	the	dell		the	far	mer	in	the	dell
3	4	4	4	4	4		4	5	5	5	5	5
O	O	O	O	O	O		I	O	O	O	O	O

hi	ho	the	der	ri	o	the	far	mer	in	the	dell
6	6	6	6	5	4	4	5	5	4	4	4
O	O	I	O	O	O	I	O	O	I	I	O

Beethoven's Ninth Symphony, known as the **Ode To Joy**, has one new type of rhythm notation. Whenever you see a small dot placed after a note, it means that you must play that note for one and a half times as long as usual. Once again, if you listen to me do it, you will hear how it should sound.

Oh When The Saints Go Marchin' In is a song that I like to improvise on, even though it is not really a blues song. I usually improvise on the notes that are held for a long time. I do this by articulating in different ways. If you would like to articulate the combinations of 6 Out notes differently than I did, please go ahead and make up some articulations of your own. Improvise! And don't let that little half beat rest (it looks a bit like a backward r) confuse you. Just listen to me play, and you will understand the timing.

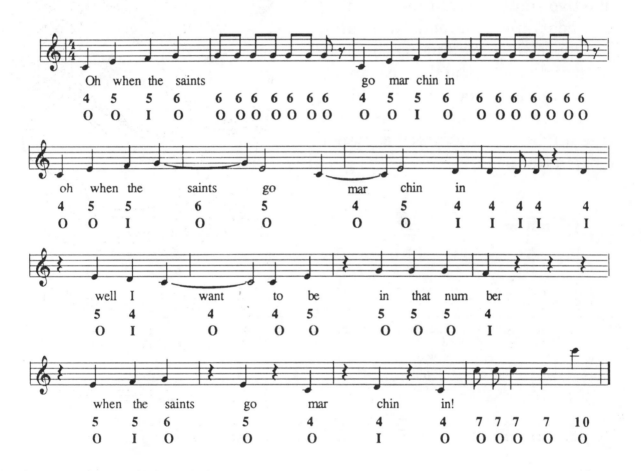

On Top Of Old Smoky

has some very long notes. Some of them are as long as seven beats, and they are held together by beams. If you run out of breath in the middle of a long note, just take a quick breath and keep playing until the end of the note. This song also has what look like two short bars at the beginning (one beat) and at the end (two beats). But since we start singing the next verse right away, the short bar in the beginning is added on to the short bar at the end to make one full bar. One full bar is only three beats, not four, in this song.

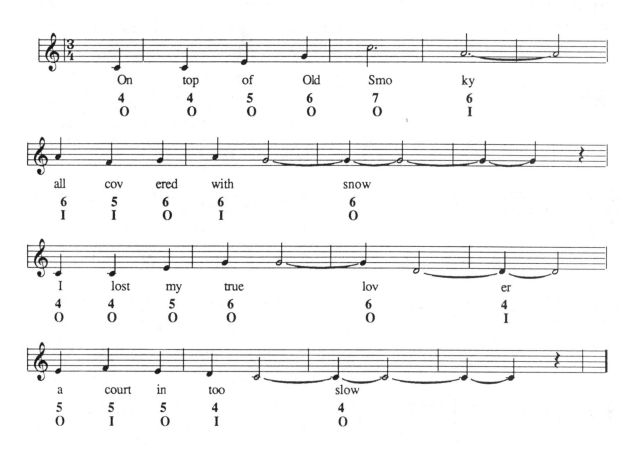

On	top	of	Old	Smo	ky
4	4	5	6	7	6
O	O	O	O	O	I

all	cov	ered	with	snow
6	5	6	6	6
I	I	O	I	O

I	lost	my	true	lov	er
4	4	5	6	6	4
O	O	O	O	O	I

a	court	in	too	slow
5	5	5	4	4
O	I	O	I	O

Lesson Eighteen: The Minor Scale

Would you like to listen to me play a minor scale?

Some people think it sounds a little bit sadder than the major scale.

What do you think?

Now I will play a song that uses the minor scale.

Please listen to Lesson Number Eighteen on the tape.

In Lesson Number Thirteen I told you about the minor scale. Now it is time to learn to play one. The A minor scale is the easiest minor scale to play. Please practice playing the A minor scale for a few minutes, and then try to play *Greensleeves*. I have changed two of the notes in *Greensleeves*. so that you do not have to bend notes.

Lesson Nineteen: Playing By Ear

Sometimes we play songs without reading music.

We call this "playing by ear".

Playing by ear is easy on the harmonica.

I will tell you how to do it.

Please listen to Lesson Number Nineteen on the tape.

The hardest part about playing a song by ear is deciding which note to begin on. I will give you the first note of some songs. You will try to figure out the rest of the song. Here's how to do it.

Play the major scale a few times before you try to figure out the notes of the song. Then play the first note of the song that I've given you. Try to sing the next note, or the next few notes. Ask yourself if the next note sounds higher or lower than the first note. Then just try to play another note on the harmonica. If it sounds right, write it down in harmonica tablature so that you will remember it. If it sounds wrong, try again. Eventually you will find the correct next note. Do this until you have written down the whole song.

At the bottom of the page I have written the first few notes of each song upside-down. If you cannot figure out these songs from just the first note, it may help to play the first few notes. But try it with just the first note, for a while.

A. Row Row Row Your Boat (begins on 4 Out)

B. Blowin' In The Wind (begins on 6 Out)

C. Puff The Magic Dragon (begins on 7 Out)

D. Happy Birthday (begins on 6 Out)

E. Michael Row (begins on 4 Out)

F. Home On The Range (begins on 6 Out)

G. Silent Night (begins on 6 Out)

H. Old Folks At Home (begins on 5 Out)

If you are trying to learn a song, and you don't know the first note, pick one of the Out notes between 4 and 7. Then try to find the next few notes. If you just can't seem to find them, pick another note to begin on.

Remember, the only complete major scale is between holes 4 and 7. Sometimes you will not be able to find a note that you need between holes 1 and 4, or between holes 7 and 10. If that happens, you probably began the song on 4 Out when you should have begun it on 7 Out.

Grown Up Helpers: Some young children seem able to play by ear surprisingly well. Perhaps the easiest way to help them develop this skill is for you to play one of the upside-down song fragments, then use the trial and error method to select a possible next note. Play it, and ask them if it sounds right or not. And remember: listening to the major scale repeatedly, and playing it, will help you both play by ear!

A.

	Row	row	row	your	boat
Breath	O	O	O	I	O
Hole	4	4	4	4	5

B.

	How	ma	ny	roads
Breath	O	O	O	I
Hole	6	6	6	6

C.

	Puff	the	ma	gic	dra	gon
Breath	O	O	O	O	I	O
Hole	7	7	7	7	7	6

D.

	Hap	py	birth	day
Breath	O	O	I	O
Hole	6	6	6	6

E.

	Mich	ael	row	the	boat	a	shore,	hal	le	lu	yah
Breath	O	O	O	O	O	I	O	O	O	I	O
Hole	4	5	6	5	6	6	6	5	6	6	6

F.

	Oh	give	me	a	home
Breath	O	O	O	I	O
Hole	6	6	7	8	8

G.

	Si	lent	night
Breath	O	I	O	O
Hole	6	6	6	5

H.

	Way	down	u	pon	the	Swan	ee	Riv	er
Breath	O	I	O	O	I	O	O	I	O
Hole	5	4	4	5	4	4	7	6	7

Lesson Twenty: Playing Along With Chords

Sometimes we like to play harmonica all by ourselves.

Sometimes we like to play along with other people.

I like to play my harmonica along with a guitar player.

It is fun and easy to do.

Please listen to cassette Lesson Number Twenty now.

You have already done some jamming, or improvising, in Lessons Number Nine, Ten, and Eleven. In those lessons you were jamming along with my synthesizer. I was only playing one chord for you to jamm along with. In Lesson Number Nine, I just played a C chord, and you just used Out notes. In Lesson Number Ten, I just played a D chord, and you just used the In notes from 4 to 10.

In the new type of jamm that we will do now, I will play you two chords to jamm along with. One is old and one is new. The old chord is the C chord. You will use the Out notes when I play the C chords, just like in Lesson Number Nine. The new chord is a G chord. You can use any of the In notes when I play the G chords. This type of jamming is called "jamming along with a chord structure". I will create a structure of C and G chords for you to jamm along with.

The chord structure that I will play for you is the same chord structure that we use to play along with the song *"Skip To My Lou"*. In fact, you may want to go back to Lesson Number Fifteen and practice that song. Then you can play it along with me.

This chord structure is 32 beats long. We can also say that it is eight bars long, since each bar equals four beats, and 32 divided by four equals eight. If we want, we can make a whole song by playing our chord structure over and over. Each time we play one of these 32 beat structures, it is called one **verse**.

Instead of just playing the notes of *"Skip To My Lou"*, try jamming along with each chord. You can jamm by using two rules. The C chord rule tells you to use any of the Out notes during the C chords. The G chord rule tells you to use any of the In notes during the G chords. Listen to my examples, then try some of your own. Here is a chart that represents this chord structure, and tells you when to use In or Out notes.

Skip To My Lou Type Eight Bar Chord Structure

● ● ● ●   ● ● ● ●   ● ● ● ●   ● ● ● ●
C chord for 8 beats   G chord for 8 beats

● ● ● ●   ● ● ● ●   ● ● ● ●   ● ● ● ●
C chord for 8 beats   G chord   C chord
                            for   for
                           4 beats   4 beats

> C chord rule: use any Out notes
> G chord rule: use any In notes

Grown Up Helpers: Practice the C and G chord rules, so that your youngster can follow them without confusion whenever you call them out (or I do). If it seems necessary, practice using one hand signal for the C chord rule (pointing your hand away from your mouth, to indicate an Out breath) and one for the G chord rule (pointing your hand in towards your mouth, to indicate an in breath). Then help him or her play along with my music and spoken instructions.

Lesson Twenty One: Jamming The Blues!

I love to play all kinds of music.

But I think that blues music is my favorite music.

Now I will teach you to play the blues.

Just listen to me play the guitar.

Listen to what I say on the tape.

I'll tell you when to breath in and when to breath out.

Then you will be playing the blues along with me!

In the last lesson, we learned to jamm along with a simple C and G chord structure. Now we will learn to jamm along with a blues chord structure. Almost all blues music uses the same chord structure. This chord structure is called the **Twelve Bar Blues Structure** because it is twelve bars, or 48 beats, long.

The Twelve Bar Blues Structure uses our old friends the C and G chords, plus a D chord. We have already jammed along with a D chord in Lesson Number Ten. You can jamm along with the blues structure by using three rules. The C chord rule tells you to use any of the Out notes during the C chords. The G chord rule tells you to use any of the In notes during the G chords. The D chord rule tells you to use any of the In notes from 4 to 10 during the D chords. Here is a chart that shows the Twelve Bar Blues Chord Structure, and the chord rules. If this seems confusing now, it won't after you've listened to the tape!

If you want to play a very simple blues structure, you can just play the G chord, C chord, and D chords. Those chords are:

G = <u>123</u>   C = <u>345</u>   D = <u>45</u>
In   Out   In

One last hint: Instead of using the high In notes for the last bar of a blues, blues players often use a type of musical signal called a **turnaround**. A turnaround announces that one verse is ending, and another is about to begin. If you look at the chart of your harmonica notes on page 29, you will see that the note 1 In is the same as 4 In and 8 In. That's why we can use it during the D chord—it's a D note! We will use a couple of loud hole number 1 Ins for a turnaround. It's easier to demonstrate on the cassette then to talk more about, so listen for a while, then blow your blues away!

Twelve Bar Blues Chord Structure

● ● ● ●   ● ● ● ●   ● ● ● ●   ● ● ● ●
G chord for 16 beats

● ● ● ●   ● ● ● ●   ● ● ● ●   ● ● ● ●
C chord for 8 beats   G chord for 16 beats

● ● ● ●   ● ● ● ●   ● ● ● ●   ● ● ● ●
D chord   C chord   G chord   D chord
for   for   for   for
4 beats   4 beats   4 beats   4 beats

> **G chord rule: use any In notes**
> **C chord rule: use any Out notes**
> **D chord rule: use any In notes from 4 to 10**

Some people like to play blues music, but they do not like to improvise all the time. So I have written out the notes of my favorite easy harmonica blues song. It is called a *Boogie Woogie Blues*. We can play it by itself, or along with the blues structure.

The Boogie Woogie Style Blues were probably invented in New Orleans sometime in the early 1900's. Originally they were played on the piano. The following verse is similar to what a boogie woogie piano player plays with his or her left hand. The right hand plays improvisations based on the blues scale. These improvisations might be made up of many notes. These long pieces of improvisation are called **runs.** The musician might also do short sections of improvisation, called **licks** or **riffs**. You can hear me play a boogie woogie with runs and licks in Lesson Number Two.

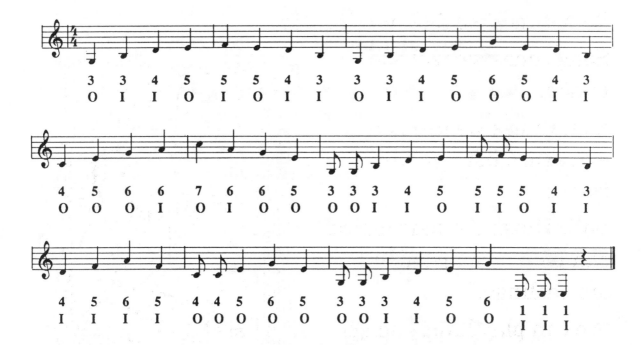

By the way: you may have noticed that the note 3 Out is the same as the note 2 In. If you like, you can substitute 2 In for the 3 Outs in the Boogie Woogie. But be careful, because 2 In is a hard hole to get a good sound out of. If your mouth or tongue are not very relaxed, your 2 In may sound like a sick sea lion!

Grown Up Helpers: If your young friend was able to play along with the "*Skip To My Lou*" chord structure, encourage him or her to play along with the blues. If you used hand signals before, use them here too, adding a third hand signal to indicate the D chord rule (since the D chord rule is to use the 4 to 10 In notes, a hand held high up and pointing in will work).

Lesson Twenty Two: Harmonica Feelings

Now you know how to play lots of music on the harmonica.

You can use the harmonica to express how you feel.

Sometimes we feel happy inside.

Sometimes we feel sad inside.

Sometimes we are not even sure how we feel inside.

Sometimes the harmonica can help us learn about our feelings.

We can play happy songs when we are happy.

We can play sad songs when we are sad.

Sometimes we can just play and see what comes out.

The harmonica has been my good friend for more than half of my life.

I hope that your harmonica will be a good friend for you, always.

This is the end of my book.

I hope that you enjoyed reading it.

Would you like to write to me?

I really like to get letters from my readers!

Goodbye now. And keep on making music!

There are two last things that I would like to tell you about.

Please practice **harmonica etiquette**. Etiquette means politeness, and politeness means that you try not to play when it will bother anyone else. Most people will enjoy hearing you play. But try to be sensitive to other peoples' feelings, especially in crowded places, or at night. Remember, you can always play very quietly. Just don't use much air!

And if you liked the blues harmonica parts of this book, you might want to learn more about it. I have a book and tape for grown ups that you are ready to use now. When you are finished with my *Instant Blues Harmonica Volume One*, I have three more advanced books and tapes! Or you can learn to play blues harmonica by listening to records, and just playing lots by yourself. I also have books called *Instant Flute* and *Instant Guitar*. They are easy to use, and lots of fun if you would like to play more instruments.

That's all for now. Please write to me. I would like to hear from you!